How to Become a Master Handgunner

D0663757

How to Become a
Master
Handgunner

The Mechanics of
X-Count Shooting

Charles Stephens

PALADIN PRESS
BOULDER, COLORADO

Also by Charles Stephens:

Advanced Master Handgunning: Secrets and
   Surefire Techniques to Make You a Winner
Cowboy Action Pistol Shooting: Secrets of Fast and
   Accurate Gunplay
Cowboy Action Rifle Shooting: Winning Techniques
   for Western Competition
Sharpshooters: How to Stand and Shoot Handgun
   Metallic Silhouettes
Thompson/Center Contender Pistol: How to Tune,
   Time, Load, and Shoot for Accuracy

How to Become a Master Handgunner:
The Mechanics of X-Count Shooting
by Charles Stephens

Copyright © 1993 by Charles Stephens

ISBN 0-87364-709-2
Printed in the United States of America

Published by Paladin Press, a division of
Paladin Enterprises, Inc.
Gunbarrel Tech Center
7077 Winchester Circle
Boulder, Colorado 80301 USA
+1.303.443.7250

Direct inquiries and/or orders to the above address.

Visit our Web site at www.paladin-press.com

To Major Golden, who encouraged me to shoot the revolver in competition again.

CONTENTS

1   Introduction

5   A Winning Grip

13   Aim at the Box While You Pull the Trigger

19   Optical Focus and Controlled Movement

25   The Shooter's Stance

33   Following Through and Calling Your Shot

39   Real-Time Shooting Diagnostics

45   Applications for X-Count Mechanics

Today's pistols are more powerful and accurate—and the handgunners that shoot them are more highly skilled—than ever before. Also, handgunners are competing in organized shooting events in ever-increasing numbers. Regardless of the above statistics, one fact has remained constant throughout the past decade: the overall percentage of shooters who are master handgunners has not changed.

Oh, new master handgunners appear on the competition scene and in the winner's circle each year, but the overall number of shooters also increases yearly. The paramount change each year is in the accuracy department.

INTRODUCTION

The few master handgunners that exist just get better at their business as time goes on. The Bianchi Cup has been shot perfectly only three times, and all were shot clean three years in a row beginning with 1990. The Speed Challenge, the Masters, and the International Practical Shooting Confederation (IPSC) Nationals are made more difficult each year, but the master handgunners continue to shoot these events faster, and with greater accuracy, than ever before. The National Rifle Association (NRA) and International Handgun Metallic Silhouette Association (IHMSA) national championship events are experiencing similar phenomena.

Guns are being made more accurate by the development of factory custom shops, whose gunsmiths fine-tune and build into each pistol every ounce of accuracy that is possible. There are more professional shooters offering training schools for both new and older shooters than ever before. Still, the sport suffers from a malady: there are just too few master handgunners for the total number of shooters competing in the sport.

When you consider how simple and uncomplicated handgun shooting is, and how easy it is to learn the basics and apply them, it is unfortunate that so few handgunners master this sport. Certain coaches who teach the game today must shoulder some blame for this deficiency. These coaches just do not teach "X-count" mechanics to their students. They teach a basic regimen that allows the student shooter to shoot seventieth- to eightieth-percentile scores at best. There is just no valid reason for these coaches not to teach the mechanics of accurate shooting.

This book is about X-count mechanics. If student shooters will read it, study it, and practice the shooting mechanics presented, they may become new statistics. They may have the opportunity to increase the percentage of shooters who become master handgunners.

The X-count mechanics presented in this book are not entirely new, and some may be considered unorthodox. However, every master handgunner actively shooting today applies some or all of them when shooting a handgun. The technique of applying a moderate grip to the pistol and then *holding that grip* as though clamping the gun in a vise may be new, although some handgunners may have been using this grip all along without fully understanding exactly what they were doing.

The idea of focusing on the front sight certainly is not new. Along with the *winning grip*, the *ability to know* when you are *not focusing* on the front sight is perhaps the most important mechanic of handgun shooting. These and other mechanics of X-count shooting, are presented in this book in the best way for you to learn them.

This book is written in the form of a tutorial. The important ideas are explained in simple terms and are often repeated so that the shooter will find the material easy to read and understand. Repeating certain terms over and over also makes the material easier to remember. The author hopes every reader will review each chapter again and again until the material has been committed to memory and fully understood. An understanding of these mechanics, along with desire and dedication, will help you succeed in becoming a master handgunner.

Before continuing to read this book, you

need to understand a few words of caution. *Always* Anytime you handle a firearm, regardless of check the how familiar you have become with it, *always* pistol and treat it as though it is loaded and, therefore, make sure it dangerous to life and limb. *Always* check a pis- is unloaded. tol to see if it is unloaded before handling it. *Always* point the gun toward the target, *down-range*, before placing your trigger finger within the trigger guard. *Never* point the firearm at another person unless you intend to shoot.

Throughout this chapter and the rest of this book I will make many references to particular types of pistols, such as revolvers and semiautos. All of the X-count mechanics that I will describe in detail are applicable to many types of pistols. For convenience, I will usually refer to only one type of pistol, such as the revolver, when describing a specific principle, technique, or mechanic.

Of all the mechanics of shooting, the shooter's grip on the pistol is the most important. If the grip is perfect, the shooter has a chance to shoot a perfect score. If it is not perfect, the shooter probably has no chance at all to shoot a perfect score. A perfect grip is one that safely controls the gun during recoil and holds it steady

A WINNING GRIP

while the sights are properly aligned during the time the trigger is pulled. The gripstocks on the gun itself must also fit perfectly, or as near so as possible, to the hand that grips them.

To grip the pistol correctly, hold the barrel (with the muzzle pointed in a safe direction after you have unloaded it) with the weak hand and slip the gun into your strong hand (the right if you are right-handed). Center the backstrap of the gun in the center of your palm. Put your trigger finger on the trigger.

Your trigger finger should touch the trigger with the center of the first finger pad. Take two narrow strips of tape, about 2 inches long and 1/8 inch wide, and tape them around the trigger finger on each side of the first finger pad. Leave just enough space between these strips of tape for the trigger to fit into cleanly. If your trigger does not fit between the strips of tape, adjust your grip on the gun so that it does. While practicing or competing, you may or may not wish to use the tape; its primary purpose is the initial learning of the winning grip.

The lower three fingers should reach around the gripstocks of the gun only so far as they are allowed as the trigger finger correctly engages the trigger. Place the thumb up high and along the left side of the revolver frame, but not so far forward that it touches the cylinder. The end pad of the thumb should not even touch the gun, but the lower joint of the thumb should. This touching of the lower thumb joint to the gun will help to ensure that the meaty base of the thumb and the part of the hand it is attached to become a primary part of the shooter's grip.

Always move the grip up as high on the backstrap as possible without touching the hammer. This allows a grip that is more in line with the bore of the barrel, as well as giving the shooter a reference point whereby he can "look" the gun into the hand each time he grips the pistol.

You may have to make small adjustments to the above description of taking the grip. No two people have exactly the same size hands. The important thing to remember in adjusting your grip is that it must feel comfortable. The center of the end pad of the trigger finger must also press or pull the trigger straight back toward the center of the palm of the hand. This straight back press or pull must be on a line with the axis of the bore of the barrel. If it isn't, the muzzle of the barrel will move slightly as the hammer falls. This will cause a shot that will usually not hit the point of aim on the target. It will not be an X-count.

Most shooters who are not masters of the sport do not know how hard to grip the pistol. The gun is not a golf club, a baseball bat, or a hammer. It must be gripped with a *moderate* amount of pressure. How much is a moderate amount? It's as strong as you can grip the gun without causing the muscles of the hand to shake the muzzle.

Where does a shooter apply this moderate pressure? On the sides of the gripstocks? NO! The pressure must be applied along the axis of the bore of the barrel. The only parts of the hand that apply pressure to the gun are the third and fourth fingers of the strong hand.

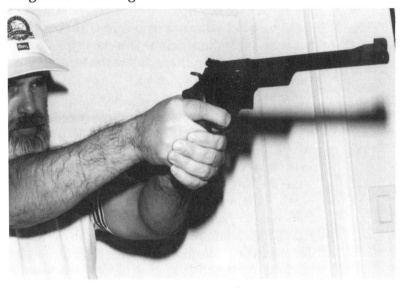

The strong hand should act like a vise, with the third and fourth fingers behaving like the moving jaws. These jaw fingers press toward the center of the pistol backstrap or the center of the palm. No pressure is applied to the gun by any other part of the hand.

Fingers of both hands press straight back using moderate pressure.

As you hold the barrel of the pistol with the weak hand, fit the gun into your strong hand. Place the web of the hand, or the part that forms a "V" between the thumb and the trigger finger, in the center of the gun's backstrap. Move the fingers of the strong hand along the right side of the pistol and curl them around the gripstrap below the trigger guard, just far enough for the center of the pad on the end joint of the trigger finger to contact the trigger. Press toward the backstrap with your third and fourth fingers using a *moderate* amount of pressure. Now hold that grip pressure; neither apply any more nor release any. Just *hold what you have.*

A Winning Grip

If you are shooting one-handed bull's-eye, then you do nothing more to your grip. If you are shooting any game that allows two-handed shooting, now is the time for the weak hand to play its part in the grip.

If you hold your hands out in front of your face with the palms facing you, the heel of each hand is that portion that adjoins the wrist. Hold your hands in front of you with the palms together. Adjust your hands so that they are perfectly aligned, with the thumbs, the index fingers, and so forth touching. Point the fingers away from you with the thumbs pointing upward. Now slide the weak hand (the left if you are right-handed) down the strong one by one finger's width. The heels of the hands should still be aligned and touching, but the index finger of the weak hand should now be lined up with the middle finger of the strong hand. Now slide the weak hand forward about 1/2 inch. Curl the lower three fingers of the strong hand inward, and then curl the first three fingers of the weak hand around these. Your trigger finger should still be pointing straight ahead. Point the thumbs forward just enough to feel relaxed, and bend the trigger finger inward as though the first pad were touching the trigger. This is the position your hands should be in when you have the proper grip on your pistol while using both hands.

How hard should you grip with the weak hand? Apply the same *moderate* pressure that you used with the strong hand. The only part of the weak hand that applies any pressure are the first three fingers. No pressure is applied by the ends of the thumbs or the little fingers of either hand. Although the heels of the hands touch each other, the weak hand is slightly to the left of the center of the gripstrap. The heels form the stationary jaws of the vise. They do not apply any pressure.

The fingers of both hands should apply pressure straight to the rear, as though they were trying to touch the center of the backstrap. This pressure should be applied when the initial grip on the gun is taken and then held. The secret to a winning grip is *maintaining* a constant grip pressure. Remember to take your grip on the pistol, apply your grip pressure with your fingers, then *hold what you have.*

The conditioning of the muscles in your hands and fingers will determine the moderate amount of grip pressure you can apply to the gun before the muzzle begins to shake. The stronger these muscles are, the stronger this moderate grip will

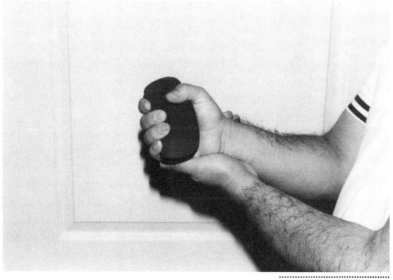

become. Used regularly, a handball or any one of several hand conditioner squeezers available at most sporting goods stores can be used regularly to build up the hand and finger muscles. Actual and dry-firing of the pistol will also help to condition these muscles. There is no physical conditioning program that will help your X-count more than time spent conditioning the hand and finger muscles.

When I see a movie star acting the part of the shooter, whether the movie is an Old West drama or a modern adventure, I always notice his or her

Condition the hand muscles by using a squeezer regularly.

A Winning Grip

grip on the gun. Most actors just do not know how to grip a pistol—or shoot one, for that matter. Should they ever have to defend themselves or their loved ones, I hope they have a baseball bat handy and not a pistol!

Unfortunately, a lot of competition pistol shooters that I observe almost daily do not know how to grip the gun properly either. An improper grip can be seen easily, as there is only one correct grip—*the winning grip*. With plenty of practice, this winning grip will become automatic. You will become so familiar with it that you will be able to grip the gun without giving the process much thought.

If you are to apply the winning grip, the gripstocks on the pistol will have to fit your hands. How will you know if they do? That's easy. If you can grip the pistol with the grip I have described and it feels comfortable, then the gripstocks probably fit your hands.

If you are unable to take the grip on the gun that I have described because your hands are too large or small, then you need to change the gripstocks on your pistol. The other test of properly fit gripstocks is the ability to put all of your shots in the X-count area of the target! Of course, you must also be able to perform all of the other mechanics correctly, too.

In summary, a winning grip is the only grip to use on a pistol. No other grip will allow you to shoot all of your shots in the X-count area of the target. The winning grip is one in which the weak hand is used to fit the pistol into the strong hand. The fingers of the strong hand and the weak hand press straight back toward the center of the backstrap with a *moderate* amount of pressure. The little fingers and the end joints of the thumbs do not apply any pressure to the pistol; nor does any other part of the hand. The heels of the hands touch slightly to the left of the center of the backstrap.

The grip is as high on the pistol as it can be without touching the hammer of the revolver, while still feeling comfortable to the shooter. If the grip does not feel comfortable during a practice session, make adjustments so that it does. Once you have your comfortable winning grip, do not change it again. Likewise, once you have a set of gripstocks on the pistol that fit your hands, do not buy another set just because some company reinvents the wheel every year.

The winning grip is the only correct grip to use, and it is the only one with which you can shoot a perfect X-count. No gimmicks, slick shortcuts, or other miracles can consistently give you high or perfect X-counts. The winning grip applies sound principles and force vectors to the grip. Learn this grip well enough so that it requires no conscious thought. You will have learned one of the most important mechanics of X-count shooting.

Early in my shooting career, I was told to aim at the X-ring of the bull's-eye. While trying to hold my sight alignment on such a small sight picture, I saw a great deal of sight movement around the small part of the target that my coach told me was my aiming point. I would press the trigger when the sights were aligned on this aiming point, then I would stop pressing the trigger when the sights drifted out of the X-ring. It seemed like an eternity until the gun would fire. Sometimes I would help the trigger by giving it a little nudge as I was running out of air. The result, very predictably, would be a miss.

Some shooters give up at this stage of the game. Others go on to become good shots using this technique of aiming at a small point on the target and pulling the trigger in small

AIM AT THE BOX WHILE YOU PULL THE TRIGGER

stages until it goes off. As far as I know, none of these students ever achieves the goal of becoming a master handgunner.

If you want all of your shots to be X-counts, you just can't aim at a small area and squeeze and hold, press and hold, and pull and hold the trigger. So if you want to be able to shoot higher scores than 70 or 80 percent, you are going to have to do it my way—the X-count way.

The best way to begin to learn the mechanics of this new "aim at the box while you pull the trigger" method is to begin by aiming at an imaginary box that makes up part of the target. Look at your target and picture a box that surrounds it. The entire box will now be your aiming point. As long as your sights are pointed in the central area of this aiming box and your trigger pull is near perfect, your shot should be an X-count.

We need to do a little dry-fire exercise at this

point in your training. Make sure your pistol is unloaded, then take your correct grip on the gun and aim at the wall in front of you. Look at the sight alignment to see that it is correct. The top of the front sight should be even with the top of the rear sight, and the front sight should be centered in the rear sight notch with an equal amount of light on each side. Focus your attention and your eyes on the front sight and touch the trigger. Now press the trigger with the index finger using a movement I call the "water-bucket pull."

The water-bucket pull goes back to the days before we all had running water in our homes. Almost every household got water from its own water well. Each well had a framework above it that held a long rope and a bucket. You lowered the bucket into the well by simply releasing the rope and letting the bucket drop down until it hit water and submerged.

When you heard the final gurgle of water rush into the bucket and knew it was filled, you grabbed the rope and took up the slack. Then you pulled with both hands using a movement called the water-bucket pull: after taking up the slack, you pulled the first foot of the rope gently, then increased the force of pull on the rope until you reached the maximum stretch length of your arms. At this point, while holding the rope with one hand, you reached as far up the rope as your arm allowed and grabbed hold of it again with your other hand. At this point, you released your hand from the lower part of the rope and reached up and took another grip high up. You repeated the water-bucket pull until you had all the water you wanted.

The secret to the water-bucket pull was the way you increased the force of your pull on the rope. You do the same thing with your trigger pull. First you touch the trigger with your finger, take up the slack (known as "travel"), then press the trigger by increasing the amount of pressure on it until the hammer falls. The trigger press is applied in one movement of the finger. This movement is as swift as the shooting game or situation demands it to be. One thing is not done, and that is pulling the trigger in stages and holding it until the sight picture is perfectly aligned on some small part of the target before applying more pressure.

The water-bucket pull is a smooth pull all the way through. You do not jerk the rope and you do not jerk the trigger. Once you decide to press the trigger, you pull it all the way through with an increasing amount of pressure until the gun fires. No other trigger pull will give you a hit on the center of the target each time. Only the water-bucket pull will provide you with an X-count each time the gun fires.

The trigger finger pulls in one continuous movement.

This water-bucket pull on the trigger is only made possible by aiming *near the central area* of your imaginary box surrounding the target rather than at a small point, such as the X-ring or the bottom edge of the target, known as "six o'clock." After you have practiced your trigger pull on the wall in your room many times and you are satis-

Aim at the Box While You Pull the Trigger

15

fied that you have this important mechanic down pat, then, and only then, tape up a target to aim *near the general area of its center.*

Again, make sure your pistol is not loaded. Take your correct grip and bring the pistol up so that the sights are aligned just under the target. While breathing with your normal rhythm, bring the pistol up so that the sights are aligned just inside of the bottom of the target. Now take a full breath of air, let about half of it out, and, while still focused on the sight alignment and particularly the top of the front sight, touch the trigger and take up any slack. Take another good breath of air and let half of it out. Check your sight alignment and focus again on the top of the front sight. Move the sight alignment toward the center of the imaginary box that surrounds the target and press the trigger with increasing pressure in one smooth movement. Focus on the front sight until the hammer falls. Watch the sights. Did they move when the hammer fell? If you did not notice any movement, you just had an X-count hit.

Does box aiming really give you more X-count hits? I have aimed at a small area, such as the bottom edge of a bull's-eye target, and shot a 7-inch group at 50 yards while standing. I have then aimed in the central area of the imaginary box surrounding the same target and shot an X-count group of 3 inches. Believe me, it works, and it works well!

Try this same experiment at your shooting range with live ammunition to see just how much better it works to aim inside the box as opposed to aiming at a small point on the same target. You, too, will be convinced to aim at a large, box-shaped area and use the water-bucket pull on the trigger.

If you have been taught by some coach, or coaches, to aim at a small point on the target, you have been trying to do something that is just not possible. A golfer does not aim at the center of the cup when he putts the ball (not if he wants to get his ball very close to the cup, he doesn't). He imagines a large, washtub-size area surrounding the cup. His aim for a 40-foot putt is the *central area* of this large washtub. For a 4-foot putt, he imagines a 9-inch paper plate surrounding the cup and aims for the *central area* of this imaginary plate.

The size of the shooter's imaginary aiming box will be determined by his ability to hold steady on a general area of a particular size. As he matures as a shooter through individual skill and practice, his ability to hold steady will improve. His imaginary box will decrease in size to match the improved ability to hold steady.

Once you gain confidence, through practice and match competition, in your ability to hit the target every time your sights are aligned within your aiming box, then you have taken a big step toward improving your X-count. By gaining this confidence, you will now focus your attention on your sights instead of some small point on the target.

Your impulse to nudge the trigger in order to make the gun fire exactly when your sights are perfectly aligned on the X-ring, or some other small point on the target, is no longer in your bag of tricks. Your reluctance to pull the trigger when you have a perfect sight picture because you're afraid you'll disturb the sights will be gone.

Don't limit all your practice sessions, dry- or live-fire, to actual targets you shoot in match competition. Do a lot of dry-fire practice on a large, blank target that has no X-count or other scoring rings. Do a lot of trigger-pull practice on the blank wall of your favorite room of the house. Remember, the larger the aiming box, the smoother the water-bucket trigger pull. You will soon be on your way toward perfect X-count shooting.

No other coordination of eyes, fingers, and

mind is more important, and none is more difficult, than that required to produce a good aim and smooth trigger release upon demand. This required coordination is the most difficult X-count mechanic to master. It just doesn't get any more difficult, and it doesn't get any easier during your shooting career.

Throughout the lifetime of your shooting, you will have to practice continually the routine of aiming within the box and pulling the trigger using the water-bucket pull. The moment you stop the practice, your X-count will drop. You may be able to shoot good scores, but you probably will not be able to shoot winning scores with the highest of X-counts unless you keep up the practice of this important mechanic.

In the last chapter I talked about aligning the sights and moving them up to a point just above the six o'clock mark inside the aiming box. As you take another breath at this moment in the shooting sequence, hold enough air in your lungs to feel comfortable, then slowly move your sight alignment up into the *central area of the of the aiming box*. This movement of the sight alignment should be slow or fast, depending on the time requirements of the particular competition you are shooting.

Whether slow or rapid, the sight movement must be deliberate and controlled, because it is during this movement that you not only take up the slack of the trigger, but you also begin to increase your pressure on the trigger. You do not wait until the aligned sights are in the center of the box to press the trigger; to do so is to invite trouble—trouble by the name of "chicken of the finger," or whatever else you may have heard it called, such as plain old "choking" or "freezing" on the target.

OPTICAL FOCUS AND CONTROLLED MOVEMENT

Whatever you call it, the result is usually the same. You either nudge the trigger quickly while the sights are holding steady on the center of the target, or you do nothing and run out of air. The consequence of these actions is almost certainly not going to be an X-count shot. To get that X-count, you must coordinate your water-bucket pull of the trigger with your controlled sight alignment movement into the *central area of the aiming box*. When you do this, you get an X-count every time. You shoot a great score and become a member of the fraternity of master handgunners.

A batter doesn't wait to swing the bat until the moment the ball reaches the plate; why should a pistol shooter wait until the aligned sights arrive at the center of the aiming box before pulling the trigger? If the batter waits until the ball arrives at the plate to start his swing, he will be way behind and will almost certainly strike out. If he is lucky, he may hit a foul ball. The pistol shooter who waits too late to begin his trigger pull will also get an egg for his trouble.

You must simply anticipate what is going to happen before it actually happens. Athletes do

The initial movement of the sights toward the target's center provides the mental signal to pull the trigger.

this all the time while playing their games. A pistol shooter is also an athlete. Train enough so that the trigger pull becomes automatic. You no longer have to think about it in order to do it.

Let the start of the controlled movement of the sight alignment in the aiming box control the start of your trigger pull. Just train enough to acquire the confidence that it will happen and it will. Let the *initial movement* of the sights toward the *central area of the the aiming box* be the mental signal that tells your trigger finger to start your *water-bucket pull.*

Train the trigger finger to let the controlled movement of the sights actually pull the trigger for you. By freeing your conscious mind of the intricate details of pulling the trigger, you can focus all your attention on the sights. You will never get "chicken of the finger."

All of your attention should be focused on the sight alignment, and mostly on the top of your front sight. Once you have trained your hands to grip the pistol, trained your controlled movement of the sight alignment to pull the trigger for you, then all you have to do to get an X-count is focus on the top of the front sight. What other sport requires you to consciously do only one thing? Take a few moments and think about this possibility. Shooting is so simple and uncomplicated that it can be done perfectly by consciously doing only one thing: *focusing on the front sight.*

It is physically impossible to focus optically on more than one object at the same time. When you focus on one object in one focal plane, everything else in all other focal planes becomes fuzzy to the eyes.

This point is *extremely* important. If you believe you are focusing on your front sight, and while doing so it becomes fuzzy, stop your shooting sequence. Start all over from the beginning. If you are running out of time, shift your attention

The optical focus must be on the front sight.

to the rear sight until it becomes very sharp and *in focus*.

Once the rear sight becomes very sharp optically, shift your focus back to the front sight and confirm your sight alignment. When your front sight becomes very sharp and *in focus*, begin your controlled movement of the sight alignment again. Your general attention is on both the target and where your sights are located on the

target, but your *optical* focus must be on the front sight. When you focus on the front sight and perform all of the other shooting mechanics well, the resulting shot will be an X-count. If your focus is on the target and your front sight is fuzzy when the gun fires, the result probably will not be an X-count.

This *focus* part of X-count mechanics is the simplest of all, because you know at all times if you are focusing on the front sight or the target. You know where your focus is because the object of this focus will be optically sharp. You know that if you focus on the front sight and not the target, the shot will be an X-count if you have performed all of the other X-count mechanics well.

The X-count choice is yours to make, and it's so simple: Don't take the shot if your front sight is fuzzy. Stop the shooting sequence, regain your focus on the front sight, then start the shooting sequence again. It's that simple.

I have placed a lot of emphasis on the front-sight focus. You must also be alert and attentive at all times to the status of your sight alignment. Don't get lazy in this department. The sight alignment is very important. If your sight alignment is perfect but your other mechanics are just a little off, the shot is probably still going to be an X-count. On the other hand, if all of your mechanics are performed perfectly and your sight alignment is off a little, the result is not going to be an X-count.

Sight alignment is like the discovery of gold. Gold and black sand are always found together. If you find gold, you will find black sand. However, if you find black sand, you will not always find gold. There are a lot of shooters who get lazy and careless with their sight alignment. Their front sight is in good focus, but the X-counts are not there!

How can you focus on the front sight and get the sight alignment exactly and precisely where you want it? You don't! This is to say that you *focus on the front sight* and *look* the sights into the *aiming box*. Once your sight alignment is confirmed and within the aiming box, you use controlled movement and *look* the optically focused front sight into the *central area* of the box. While you are using the controlled movement and maintaining your sight focus, your finger is applying an increasing amount of pressure on the trigger until the pistol fires automatically.

If you attempted to move the sight alignment or the front sight to a small, precise point on the target, your trigger finger would probably freeze on the trigger. You could not pull the trigger without some amount of conscious nudge with the finger. The resulting shot probably would not be an X-count.

Some shooters, even master handgunners, change their optical focus back and forth from the front sight to the target and back again. They are able to make the focus change to the front sight just before the trigger finger pulls the last ounce of trigger resistance and the gun fires. They have young eyes! Mine are middle-aged eyes. They are no longer elastic enough to change focus between a near object and a far object in a microsecond.

It doesn't matter how you do it. As long as your last optical focus is on the front sight and your sights are perfectly aligned at the time the gun fires, you have performed the mechanics of sight alignment and optical front-sight focus very well, and the result will be an X-count.

Training is the secret. You must train your trigger finger and your eyes to do certain simple things during the same time period. These eye and trigger finger motions may be simple, but there should not be any doubt as to how complex coordinating them during the same time period becomes. Complex actions must be practiced and their components trained in order for success to be achieved. In the chapter on dry-firing (firing by the wall), I will stress this training aspect. If you will do the practice and accomplish the training of the various body parts involved in the mechanics of shooting, you will succeed.

The shooter's stance should not be poured in cement. Most shooters will make minor changes to their stances throughout their shooting careers. Most of these subtle changes will result from physical changes to the body from aging and from muscle development as a result of exercise associated with an active shooting program. Some marked changes may result from experimentation by the shooter who is always looking for and trying out new techniques. Regardless of many changes, the shooter's stance will most likely vary with every shooter from the very beginning.

THE SHOOTER'S STANCE

There are several standing positions that are universal for shooting handguns. From these positions the individual shooter can select the one that is the most comfortable and offers the greatest stability for him.

The components involved in a shooting stance are simple, but like all other shooting mechanics, individual components must be coordinated and performed during the same time period. When people coordinate several physical and mental acts, the entire process becomes complex. The simpler the components of the stance are made, the easier it becomes for the shooter to coordinate them.

Among the components of the stance is the consistency of head placement. The face, eyes, and upper torso must be placed in the same position for every shot of a sequence of shots. The shooter's body must be placed in its natural or neutral state of standing. This neutral position must offer the shooter a natural point of aim at the target. Above all, the shooter's stance must be comfortable, relaxed, and allow unrestricted breathing.

Take the initial stance for one-handed shoot-

ing, facing the target. With the gun pointed toward the target, take your winning grip but do not place your trigger within the trigger guard or on the trigger at this time. Hold the gun at the ready position; that is, hold your gun arm's elbow against your body with the arm bent at the elbow such that the pistol is pointing in the air at about a 45-degree angle to the body. Move the left leg (if you are right-handed) to your left and to the rear, such that your toes are about 2 feet apart. Now turn your right foot so that the toe of your footgear points about 60 degrees to the left of the target. Both feet should almost be parallel to each other with the heels pointed inward just slightly. The gun should still be held at the ready position and in a line with the target. The shooter's trigger finger should still remain outside of the trigger guard and off the trigger.

Now comes one of the components of the stance that varies a lot from shooter to shooter. The weak hand, since this is one-handed shooting, must be placed somewhere. Some shooters stick the weak hand into their belts, either in back or front. Some just let it hang down by their side. I prefer to stick it into my left front pants pocket. It stays there very consistently from shot to shot, very relaxed and comfortable.

After deciding where you are going to put your weak hand initially, you are now ready to point the pistol so that the sights are properly aligned on the target. After bringing the gun down from the ready position and pointing it at the target, you should notice that the body weight is equally distributed, more or less, on both feet.

Another component of the stance that varies from shooter to shooter is the knee position. Some shooters stand with their knees locked but relaxed. I prefer to stand with my shooting arm straight, but my knees are slightly bent. This bend of my knees is so slight that you would never notice it by looking at my trousers. My right knee (I'm right-handed) is bent a little more than my left, such that my right shoulder down to my trigger finger is in a straight line with the target. My back is straight, and I try not to bend from the waist. I'm able to maintain a line of sight from my eye, across the pistol sights, and to the target aiming box because my right knee is bent a little more than my left. You don't have to do it this way. Remember, the stance is not the same for everyone, and it's not poured in cement.

If your pistol is unloaded, try several dry-fire shots within your aiming box. Find a shooting position that is comfortable and relaxed for you. This will be your natural or neutral stance. Probably the only muscle application you will feel will be in the strong forearm, from the weight of the pistol. The more dry-firing and shooting you do, along with other physical exercise, the less of this forearm muscle application you will feel.

Your breath control is an important part of your stance. As you aim your pistol within the target aiming box and breathe in a normal way, you will see the sights rise and dip above and below the target. In order to stop this rise and

The Shooter's Stance
....
27

dip of the pistol and its sights, you must hold your breath. Practice holding your breath while you aim. You will quickly find out that you are more relaxed at this respiratory pause if you let some air out and hold just a portion of it while you aim. Just how much you hold is another one of those things that varies from shooter to shooter. You have to find out which works best for you; hold a little, a lot, or just about half a breath. I find holding about two-thirds of a breath works best for me.

Adjust your stance for your natural point of aim.

Now is the time to adjust your stance for your natural point of aim. Your natural point of aim allows you to take your neutral stance, so that the least amount of muscle application is used in standing and aiming. While doing your breath routine and watching the sights rise and dip in relation to the target, close your eyes. That's right—close your eyes and move your arm with the pistol pointed toward the target to a position that feels the most relaxed and comfortable to you.

Once you have found this arm position, hold it and open your eyes. Where is the target in relation to your sight alignment? Move your left (rear) foot and pivot your right foot until the sights are aligned on target. Close your eyes once again and repeat this process until you can open your eyes and find the sights almost aligned on your target aiming box. This is your natural point of aim. Stay in this position and note where your feet are in relation to the firing line or target.

You will need to place your feet exactly as they are now, in relation to the rest of your body and the target, each time you take your stance. You have now fixed a good portion of your stance as defined by your natural point of aim and your natural or neutral position.

Regardless of the things that you will have to change in your stance as compared with another shooter, there are those components which are universally the same. Your head should be held erect and the eyes should look straight at the target. Head and eye position, in relation to the pistol sights and target, must be consistent from shot to shot or you will not shoot X-counts. Remember, this book is about X-count mechanics. If you want X-counts, you must consistently keep your head erect, with the eyes looking straight at the target aiming box.

Develop a one-arm shooting stance that gives you the stablest of platforms from which to fire the pistol. Let this be your natural or neutral stance. Now let us explore the various two-handed shooting stances.

One of the oldest of standing, two-handed pistol shooting positions is the Isosceles stance. The stance is assumed by facing the target and spreading your feet about 2 feet apart, with the toes even and pointed comfortably outward. Bring the pistol up with the sights aligned on the target. Your elbows should be locked, or almost so (according to individual preference). Bend both knees just slightly, without having to use muscle application to maintain the bend. Your

The Shooter's Stance
....
29

head should be erect and the eyes should look straight at the sights and target. That's all there is to assuming the Isosceles stance.

The Isosceles stance.

You will want to close your eyes and find your natural point of aim as before. Once found, note where your feet are located in relation to your body, the firing line, and the target. Now you have the Isosceles stance as it fits you and your neutral body stance.

Another two-handed pistol shooting stance that I like to use is the Weaver stance. To assume this stance, once again face the target and spread your feet about 2 feet apart. Move the right foot back about 6 inches and bring the gun up with the sights aligned on the target aiming box. Bend the elbows and bring the pistol in toward your chest a few inches. Your right elbow will be bent quite a bit more than your left if you are right-handed. Your knees should be locked, or almost so—whatever is comfortable to you. Whether the knees are bent or locked, the leg muscles must be relaxed.

Once again you must find your natural point of aim for the Weaver stance. When you find it,

note the positions of the feet with the body, the The Weaver stance. firing line, and the target. You will want to place them near their present location for each shot from this stance.

Always remember that the above-described shooting stances have to be adjusted by each shooter so the stance will fit the individual. This is because each shooter is an individual as far as physical size and dexterity. Regardless of how you stand while shooting the pistol, there are components of the stance that are part of X-count mechanics. These are keeping the head erect with the face square to the target and looking straight out at the target. All of the other components of the stance can be changed by the shooter, but you'd better not change the X-count mechanics. If you don't believe me, go ahead and experiment with these mechanics. You will soon find out for yourself that there really are components of the stance that are universal to all master handgunners who shoot high X-counts.

Universal
mechanics:
head erect
and eyes
looking
straight
ahead.

Why is it called dry-firing? Because you do it without any ammunition—no bang and no clank. It's dry, and to some it's boring, something to do when the weather is bad and you just don't want to go outside to shoot. But it should not have to be dry and boring. Novice and master handgunners alike continue to develop throughout their shooting careers. Dry-firing should be a major part of your shooting program, not only while you're learning X-count mechanics but throughout your development as a shooter.

Dry-firing has been important for me, as I have always used it as a tool in developing and maintaining my follow-through. Shooters will get into a rut at times during their career and begin to shoot a little, or even a lot, below their normal abilities.

FOLLOWING THROUGH AND CALLING YOUR SHOT

When I've recently fallen into such a slump and my scores have fallen off, I use dry-firing to discover why. Baseball players get into ruts with their hitting; golfers do, too. Shooters aren't not immune to such slumps, either. When this happens, it's best to have a good coach watch you shoot several shots until he can pick up on what you are doing wrong. If a shooting coach is not immediately available, there is a good possibility that you can find your problem yourself by dry-firing.

Even if you are not able to see yourself shoot, you can see your sights when you do. Dry-firing is at its best when used as a tool for finding the faults of the shooter.

Let's forget about ammunition and targets for the time being. Get your favorite pistol, unload it, and sit down in your favorite chair. Turn on enough lights in the room to illuminate a nearby wall as brightly as possible. You will need to be able to see your sight alignment as clearly as you can for this exercise.

Just think about it. You are going to find the problem that you have been plagued with recently while shooting. Dry-firing should no longer be boring. If dry-firing is so deeply rooted in memory that you cannot disassociate it from boredom, let's call it by another name. Since you are going to be firing at a wall, let's call it "wall-firing."

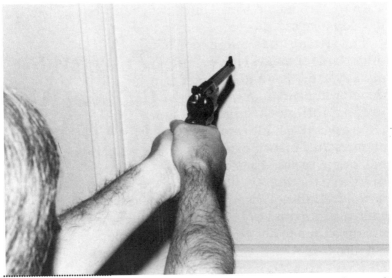

Dry- or wall-firing at a brightly lit wall.

The wall should be as free from marks and blemishes as can be. You don't want to have anything on the wall that might distract your attention from your sights. Grip your gun with the winning grip, point it at the wall, and align the sights. Look at the rear sight and describe what you see. Is it clear from scratches or dents? Have you recently sprayed it with sight black which has rubbed off in certain areas? Now look at your front sight for any abnormalities. Is it free from blemishes?

Now that we know what our sights look like today, we are ready to fire at the wall. Take your normal breath, exhale a portion of it, and align the sights. Focus on the front sight, but be attentive to how it is aligned within the rear sight. When your front sight focus is at its clearest, pull the trigger with your water-bucket pull, using an increasing trigger finger pressure. How were the sights aligned when the hammer fell? If you don't remember what the sights looked like when the hammer fell, then you have just discovered that one of your recent problems has been *follow-through.*

You may be suffering from other problems, such as heeling the pistol or dipping the front sight, at hammer-fall time. Just continue to wall-fire and focus on the front sight while being very attentive to sight alignment on the brightly lit blank wall. You should soon discover most, if not all, of your recent problem areas of shooting the pistol.

Whatever your recent problems, continue to wall-fire until you can clearly see that you are holding perfect sight alignment and that it is not disturbed at hammer fall. You should soon be seeing perfect sight alignment without having to think about trigger pull. When this happens, you will have just experienced good follow-through.

Just like ballplayers, golfers, and other athletes, a shooter must have follow-through to perform well. A lot of athletes have been taught that follow-through is done at the end of their swing or shot. If you were taught this definition, you should change it. Change the concept of follow-through to paying attention from the start to the finish of your shot sequence. Most dictionaries define *follow* as "paying attention to," and define *through* as "end to end." It's just a matter of discovering now what you should have been taught from the beginning.

Since follow-through is nothing more than paying attention to what you do with the pistol from the time you grip it until the hammer falls, what better way to develop it than firing on a brightly lit, blemish-free wall? Pay attention to your sight alignment and focus on the front sight while observing your sights outlined upon a brightly lit wall, and you will develop follow-through.

At this point, you may very well be asking yourself just exactly what it was that you were taught as follow-through with the bat when you were playing baseball as a youngster. To hit the ball well, you could not stop your swing at the moment of contact with the ball. You had to meet the ball with the bat and continue to swing through the ball. This act should have been called "swing-through," not follow-through. A baseball player follows through from the moment he sees the pitcher release the ball until he drops the bat to run to first base after the ball is hit. *That is follow-through.*

If a baseball player's act of swinging through the ball is just called *swing-through*, and the complete process of watching the pitcher release the ball through dropping the bat to the ground after hitting is his *follow-through*, what, then, do you call what the pistol shooter does after the hammer falls? This component of the shooting sequence is identified as "calling your shot."

If your focus is on the front sight, and all of your attention is on sight alignment and its relation to the aiming box at the moment of hammer fall, you will see where the bullet hits. Sometimes you will actually see the bullet hole appear in a paper target as the bullet goes through, if your total attention is devoted to what you are doing. Seeing the hole suddenly appear in the paper target is known as calling your shot.

You will not always see the bullet hole at the moment it is created. Sometimes the target will be too far away for you to see the hole, even after the bullet goes through. If your attention was devoted entirely to your shooting sequence, your eyes were optically focused on the front sight, and you were careful to pay attention to your sight alignment and its relative position inside the aiming box of the target at the moment of hammer fall, you have called your shot.

A shooter follows through as he pays attention to what he is doing from the time he grips the pistol until he has called his shot. This is *shooter follow-through*. Anything less than total awareness or attention during the shooting sequence and the shooter has not followed through. If you have performed all your other mechanics well, the result of total follow-through will be the call of your shot and an X-count.

Now that we have a new definition of follow-through and we know that complete follow-through enables a shooter to call his shot, let's discuss wall-firing again. Wall-firing can be used as a tool for doing things other than finding your shooting problems. A planned regimen of wall-firing can perfect your follow-through, enable you to call your shot, train your attention to sight alignment, train your trigger finger by teaching it the water-bucket pull, and train your hand or hands to grip the pistol correctly. The more dry-firing you do, the more you will be able to do all of the X-count mechanics without having to give each one much conscious thought.

Once you are trained well enough in the mechanics, you can just pick up the pistol and shoot. The process will become thought-free and stress-free. The entire shooting sequence will become relaxed, and your movements when shooting will flow as smoothly as Wyoming's lazy, meandering Wind River in mid-summer.

Because the end results of wall-firing are so rewarding, it is important that it become as much a part of your shooter development program as live-fire practice and match competition. Wall-firing should be scheduled ahead of time. This doesn't mean that when you have some slack time in your daily schedule you shouldn't use it for wall-firing. Just don't overdo it—physically, that is. When you are tired, rest. Don't wall-fire or live-fire when you are physically or mentally tired. Also, as you are wall firing and you reach your physical and mental limits, take a break. When you are rested, continue your practice.

Establish what it is that you want to accomplish with each wall-firing session or group of sessions. If you want to add a target to the wall for some particular need or purpose, then do so. Wall-firing is like most other tools; it is not poured into concrete. Change it any way you wish in order to meet your specific, scheduled requirements. Just remember, above all, don't wall-fire just for the sake of wall-firing. You just may get careless with your shooting mechanics if you do it with no specific purpose in mind.

Since one of the purposes of the valuable tool of wall-firing is to find faults, you certainly want to be extra cautious about wall-firing pitfalls. Should your interest just not be with the program on some days, don't think your schedule is dyed in the wool and must be done at all costs. If you know you can't pay 100-percent attention to what you are doing when you wall- or live-fire, do something else. Go fishing and just take a day off from shooting.

The number-one pitfall of wall-firing is taking it lightly. When the shooter doesn't take this tool seriously, he gets careless while using it and actually develops even more faults in the process. Wall-firing is the primary tool used to find faults and develop your follow-through from beginning to end of the shooting sequence, enabling you to call your shot. Any shooting tool used to develop X-count mechanics should be used carefully, not carelessly.

This chapter is about shooting diagnostics. This is directly related to X-count mechanics in that it allows the shooter to monitor his performance. Therefore, it is of great importance. Satisfaction is the feeling a shooter has when he sees an X-count hit on the target. Other hits on the target that are not X-counts might not give the shooter as much satisfaction, but they are just as important.

Seeing an X-count hit shows you that you did everything right. But looking at other hits outside of the X-ring or just outside of the bull can show you what you are doing wrong. Studying all of the hits on the target is the science of shooting diagnostics.

REAL-TIME SHOOTING DIAGNOSTICS

While you are shooting in real time with live ammunition, you can also see what you are doing right and wrong. The study of errors committed during real time is also a part of the science of shooting diagnostics.

Shooting diagnostics is a powerful tool with which we can analyze our performance of the mechanics of shooting. The shooter can analyze the holes in the target, along with remembering what he did as he fired the gun in real time. The science of shooting diagnostics consists of putting this information together.

Was the front sight fuzzy at the moment you fired the shot? Did you get careless with the sight alignment when you fired? If so, the holes in the target should be random misses. There should not be a cluster of shots on any one area of the target (provided you performed all of the other shooting mechanics well). The holes should be randomly dispersed over the face of the entire target, making a rather large group.

In making such a diagnosis, the shooter is assumed to have already ruled out the possibility that his pistol malfunctioned or his ammunition

was not accurate. We are discussing the science of shooting diagnostics as they relate to the performance of the shooter, and nothing else.

If your follow-through was complete and you called a shot high and above the bull on the target, and while checking the target you saw there was a bullet hole in that spot, there is no analysis to be made. You simply hit where you were aiming. If you called the shot dead center in the bull and found the hole low and left of the bull (seven to eight o'clock area), the analysis of the facts leads to the diagnosis that flinching was the cause of missing the X-ring. A good coach could watch you shoot that same shot and tell you that you jerked or nudged the trigger off in anticipation of the pistol firing (recoil).

You can read the shot on the target and make the same deduction. Before reading the target, it's best to fire several shots, which you call dead-center hits, and find them bunched or strung out toward seven to eight o'clock from the bull. Your data (holes in the target) has greater validity—and a better chance of being believed—if you fire ten shots rather than one or two.

When you called the shots dead-center, or

Careless sight alignment results in a large group.

near so, and you find holes in the target that are quite high and a little right of the bull (twelve to two o'clock), this can be diagnosed as being caused by heeling the pistol. Heeling is the result of anticipating the recoil by pushing the heel of your hand or hands forward and up while gripping the pistol. Heeling also is usually accompanied by jerking or consciously

nudging the trigger, as with flinching. (The difference between heeling and flinching is the direction in which your hands move as you anticipate the gun's recoil.)

Flinching, or jerking, the trigger results in hits out at seven o'clock.

Holes you find on the target which are just a little out of the X-ring and in the area of eight to ten o'clock, which you called dead-center, can be diagnosed as being caused by trigger finger pushing. This results from the trigger finger pushing on the right side of the trigger (if you are right-handed) instead of pressing or pulling straight back in a line toward the center of the backstrap.

Holes found clustered about an area two to four o'clock and just a little out of the X-ring, which you called dead-center hits, can usually be diagnosed as being caused by thumb pressure.

This is a result of applying pressure with the strong-hand thumb's last or end joint, or the end joints of both the weak and strong hands. Read the chapter on the winning grip again for help in correcting this problem.

The shooter is advised to apply caution to real- and post-time diagnoses, along with reading of the target. You must know that your ammuni-

Heeling results in shots out at twelve to two o'clock.

tion is accurate for your gun. You must also know the mechanical condition of your sights and pistol. Did you forget to tighten all the frame screws before shooting? I always make tightening all the screws and sights the last act of cleaning my pistol before putting it away. Some screws are even hidden from view under the gripstocks. You also might want to add this little chore to your gun cleaning procedure.

Before long you will be reading your targets and making your own shooting diagnoses. You will be able to tell exactly what you did that caused the bullet to hit where it did on the target. Being able to know which of the X-count mechanics you did wrong and which of them you did right using the science of shooting diagnosis is a powerful skill that every shooter can acquire. This book describes each of the X-count mechanics. If you find out from reading the target that you are not doing one of the mechanics correctly, just read the description of how to do it again. Do some wall-firing until you are satisfied that you have corrected your fault, or faults; then do some real-time shooting and check your results.

Simple, isn't it? Shooting good scores is simple. As long as you learn the correct way to do it, learn by calling your shots during real time, and learn to read the target and diagnose your faults, then you have no more excuses. You either devote the necessary time to become a master handgunner and remain one throughout your shooting career, or you find another sport or something else that challenges you to devote your time to.

I hope this book helps you to achieve your shooting goals. Hopefully you will share your recently acquired information with others who are also struggling to shoot more accurately with the pistol.

Pushing the trigger can result in hits out from eight to ten o'clock.

Too much
thumb pres-
sure can
cause hits
out at two
to four
o'clock.

A
ccuracy requirements are not the same for all pistol shooting games. I don't know how many times I've heard that line; it just isn't true. The common denominator for all shooting games is accuracy. Yes, accuracy is the common denominator for NRA and IPSC handgun metallic silhouette shooting, NRA Action Shooting and the Bianchi Cup, the Steel Challenge, the Master's, bull's-eye pistol matches, Practical Police Competition (PPC), and even all *air pistol* competition.

Speed (or time) requirements are not the same for all pistol shooting games. I haven't heard this statement very often, but I believe it to be true. Speed is the one element of shooting that is different for all of the above shooting

APPLICATIONS FOR X-COUNT MECHANICS

games. Never confuse speed requirements with accuracy requirements.

When you are learning these two shooting elements, you should learn and master accuracy first, then speed. Learning accuracy first will teach you the important asset of being careful. Trying to learn speed induces the pitfall of being careless. After you have learned how to be accurate with a handgun, speed will come automatically. A shooter will follow a natural progression toward shooting faster as he practices being accurate. You don't learn speed, you develop it.

Of course, there will be things that you will learn, both from other shooters and coaches and from your own experimentation, that will help you increase your efficiency of motion, which will also increase your speed. Examples of motion efficiency would be the line your hand would take from a ready position to the pistol in your holster and the line your hand would take from your grip to your spare magazine for a reload.

There are several excellent books written about practical shooting that cover the subject of motion and time efficiency. I suggest you read them after you have learned how to shoot accurately.

This chapter is on the applications of X-count mechanics in the world of shooting games and real-life situations. The mechanics of shooting, as they have been

explained and defined in this book, can be applied to the many shooting games because they have been designed for time efficiency as well as accuracy. Their application to so many games was by design and not accident.

Trigger control, as managed by the shooter while using the water-bucket pull, can be applied to slow-fire target disciplines, such as bull's-eye and handgun metallic silhouette shooting; timed-fire disciplines, such as NRA Action Pistol Shooting; and for rapid-fire disciplines, such as the Steel Challenge and IPSC matches. Trigger control, as learned by the use of the water-bucket pull, enables the shooter to press the trigger through let-off and hammer-fall *on demand*.

If the requirement is for slow-fire, intermediate- or timed-fire, or rapid-fire, the mechanics of trigger pull, as explained in this book, will work for you. They will work because you do not wait until your sights are aligned on a specific point on a target before you begin your trigger pull. Remember, you acquire your target with your sights by aligning them within an aiming box, while pulling the trigger during your controlled movement of the sights toward the central area of the aiming box.

The X-count mechanics are time-efficient and can be performed upon demand by the shooter in almost all shooting situations. If your life is in jeopardy, by using the mechanics described in this book, you could quickly dispatch an attacker with your pistol. X-count mechanics were designed to be used on demand by the shooter. Your aiming box might be the entire chest of your attacker. Your sights would be aligned very rapidly within that box, while your trigger finger applied a rapidly increasing trigger pressure to the trigger. The result would most likely be several quick shots in succession to your attacker's chest area. He would be dispatched upon demand! Remember, never point a pistol at anyone unless your life is threatened and you fully intend to shoot your attacker.

Practicing X-count mechanics during wall-fire drills will show you just how fast you can use the water-bucket pull on the trigger without disturbing or upsetting your sights or sight alignment. Just watch your sight alignment on the brightly lit blank wall while your trigger finger takes up any slack or travel. When your focus on the front sight becomes sharp, your finger will pull the trigger all the way through let-off in one smooth but rapid pull. Pull the trigger more rapidly each time, and notice how quickly you can pull it before the front sight is disturbed.

While doing your wall-fire drills, you might want to just close your eyes and get a feel for the trigger when you pull it rapidly, on demand. Just increase the pressure with your finger more rapidly each time. With your eyes closed, your mind will have less to think about during this drill. You just let your mind store up the information that your finger is sending it. Now that you know you can pull the trigger very rapidly and smoothly without disturbing your sights, you can fire the pistol without hesitation.

Practicing any of the X-count mechanics of accurate pistol shooting should prove to you that they are designed to be time-efficient. These X-count mechanics must first be learned by reading this book and then through practice. Remember, speed is not an element that can be learned. It will be developed through practice, while you are learning your shooting mechanics. The more you learn through your practice, both wall-fire and real-time shooting, the faster you will become at shooting the pistol.

When shooting handgun metallic silhouettes, you will have enough time to go through the process of taking your winning grip and stance for each shot slowly. You should use all of the available time to perform your X-count mechanics. Be careful at each step in your shooting sequence. The shooting distances to each target will be far, but the time requirements are generous. Make use of all of this time by doing everything slowly, deliberately, and carefully.

When you are shooting an individual stage during an IPSC match, remember that your mechanics you have learned can be called on demand by the shooter. Just move the pistol from target to target, aligning the sights and pulling the trigger with an increasing amount of finger pressure while you move the sights into the central area of the center of your aiming box within each target.

You don't have to move the sights (whether they are iron sights, scope, or electronic) into the aiming box from the bottom. You can move them into your aiming box from either side or the top. The direction you choose to enter the box is not dyed in the wool or sealed in cement. It is an element of motion efficiency, not a mechanic of shooting.

If you have practiced and learned well, it will be like driving a car around curve after curve on a road course or a winding mountain highway. You take each curve before thinking about the next one. You will acquire and hit each target before thinking about the next one. Your eyes will see an aiming box within or around each target, and your trigger will pull through to let-off as rapidly as you demand.

I'll never forget the time I shot so fast that I almost went into shock—from disbelief, that is. I did not *try* to shoot fast at all. I just walked up to the firing line with six steel plates 15 yards downrange. I was practicing for my first Bianchi Cup match. When the buzzer on my timer sounded, I just drew my old Colt Government Model .45 auto and moved the sights from steel target to target while applying all of my X-count mechanics.

After I shot the first two steel plates with average speed, the pistol seemed to fire by itself as I rapidly moved the sights to the next target. The same automatic fire mechanism worked until I had hit the last plate. I was shocked by the speed of the last four shots.

Knowing that I couldn't possibly have hit those targets anywhere close to center, I slowly walked toward where they lay upon the ground. To my amazement, each target had a bullet mark in almost exactly the same spot, near dead center. The gun had simply gone into automatic fire all by itself, or so I thought. I just did not expect the shots to be dead-center hits.

After resetting the steel plates and painting them, I remembered to check my timer. I stared in disbelief: the display read 2.78 seconds. It was my fastest time on the 15-yard plates to date. I really believed that my pistol had malfunctioned on that run. My mind was having a difficult time accepting the fact that I had actually fired those fast shots.

I'm sure a lot of master handgunners have experienced the same thing. I'm also sure that many of you who master the X-count mechanics will be out practicing them one day and discover that what I've said about speed really is true. *Speed will develop automatically while you are practicing to be accurate.*

An expert on handgun accuracy, national champion and master handgunner Charles (Charlie) Stephens has spent the last half of his shooting career pursuing the challenging shooting sport of long-range pistol silhouette competition. His last book, *The Sharpshooters,* was published shortly after he was awarded the Golden Ram Ring for winning the NRA National Championship in the standing aggregate event of the 1990 Long Range Pistol Metallic Silhouette Nationals. Having spent the past 10 years finding out how—and why—some shooters master this long-range pistol shooting game, Stephens reveals the winning techniques of the all-time great masters in *The Sharpshooters.*

Stephens' *How to Become a Master Handgunner* will serve

ABOUT THE AUTHOR

Author Charles (Charlie) Stephens.

as a powerful tutorial on the mechanics of accurate pistol shooting, and it will be a stepping stone for many shooters who seek perfection in performance.

Stephens resides in New Mexico, where he continues to participate in various pistol shooting competitions throughout the Southwest, while writing about shooting and hunting adventures.

If you liked this book, you will also want to read these: